Calculus methods
Unit Guide
The School Mathematics Project

CAMBRIDGE
UNIVERSITY PRESS

Main authors   Simon Baxter
Stan Dolan
Doug French
Andy Hall
Barrie Hunt
Mike Leach
Tim Lewis
Lorna Lyons
Richard Peacock
Paul Roder
Jeff Searle
David Tall
Thelma Wilson
Phil Wood

Project director   Stan Dolan

The authors would like to give special thanks to Ann White for her help in producing the trial edition and in preparing this book for publication.

Published by the Press Syndicate of the University of Cambridge
The Pitt Building, Trumpington Street, Cambridge CB2 1RP
40 West 20th Street, New York, NY 10011–4211, USA
10 Stamford Road, Oakleigh, Victoria 3166, Australia

© Cambridge University Press 1992

First published 1992

Produced by Gecko Limited, Bicester, Oxon.

Cover design by Iguana Creative Design

Printed in Great Britain at the University Press, Cambridge

British Library cataloguing in publication data

A catalogue record for this book is available from the British Library.

ISBN 0 521 40884 9

Contents

Introduction to 16–19 Mathematics

Nobody reads introductions and nobody reads teachers' guides, so what chance does the introduction to this Unit Guide have? The least we can do is to keep it short! We hope that you will find the discussion point and tasksheet commentaries and ideas on presentation and enrichment useful.

The School Mathematics Project was founded in 1961 with the purpose of improving the teaching of mathematics in schools by the provision of new course materials. SMP authors are experienced teachers and each new venture is tested by schools in a draft version before publication. Work on *16–19 Mathematics* started in 1986 and the pilot of the course has been used by over 30 schools since 1987.

Since its inception the SMP has always offered an 'after sales service' for teachers using its materials. If you have any comments on *16–19 Mathematics*, or would like advice on its use, please write to:

> 16–19 Mathematics
> The SMP Office
> The University
> Southampton SO9 5NH

Why 16–19 Mathematics?

A major problem in mathematics education is how to enable ordinary mortals to comprehend in a few years concepts which geniuses have taken centuries to develop. In theory, our view of how to pass on this body of knowledge effectively and pleasurably has changed considerably; but no great revolution in practice has been seen in sixth-form classrooms generally. We hope that in this course, the change in approach to mathematics teaching embodied in GCSE schemes will be carried forward. The principles applied in the course are appropriate to this aim.

- Students are actively involved in developing mathematical ideas.
- Premature abstraction and over-reliance on algorithms are avoided.
- Wherever possible, problems arise from, or at least relate to, everyday life.
- Appropriate use is made of modern technology such as graphic calculators and microcomputers.
- Misunderstandings are confronted and acted upon.
  By applying these principles and presenting material in an attractive way, A level mathematics is made more accessible to students and more meaningful to them as individuals. The *16–19 Mathematics* course is flexible enough to provide for the whole range of students who obtain at least a grade C at GCSE.

Structure of the courses

The A and AS level courses have a core-plus-options structure. Details of the full range of possibilities, including A and AS level *Further Mathematics* courses, may be obtained from the Joint Matriculation Board, Manchester M15 6EU.

For the A level course *Mathematics (Pure with Applications)*, students must study eight core units and a further two optional units. The structure diagram below shows how the units are related to each other. Other optional units are presently being developed to give students an opportunity to study aspects of mathematics which are appropriate to their personal interests and enthusiasms.

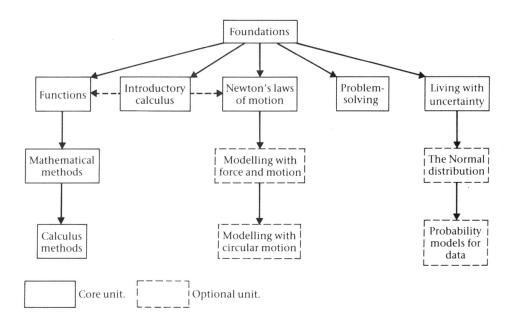

The *Foundations* unit should be started before or at the same time as any other core unit.

Any of the other units can be started at the same time as the *Foundations* unit. The second half of *Functions* requires prior coverage of *Introductory calculus*. *Newton's laws of motion* requires calculus notation which is covered in the initial chapters of *Introductory calculus*.

For the AS level *Mathematics (Pure with Applications)* course, students must study *Foundations*, *Introductory calculus* and *Functions*. Students must then study a further two applied units.

Material

The textbooks contain several new devices to aid an active style of learning.

- Topics are opened up through **group discussion points**, signalled in the text by the symbol

and enclosed in rectangular frames. These consist of pertinent questions to be discussed by students, with guidance and help from the teacher. Commentaries for discussion points are included in this unit guide.

- The text is also punctuated by **thinking points**, having the shape

and again containing questions. These should be dealt with by students without the aid of the teacher. In facing up to the challenge offered by the thinking points it is intended that students will achieve a deeper insight and understanding. A solution within the text confirms or modifies the student's response to each thinking point.

- At appropriate points in the text, students are referred to **tasksheets** which are placed at the end of the relevant chapter. A tasksheet usually consists of a self-contained piece of work which is used to investigate a concept prior to any formal exposition. In many cases, it takes up an idea raised in a discussion point, examining it in more detail and preparing the way for formal treatment. There are also **extension tasksheets** (labelled by an E), for higher attaining students, which investigate a topic in more depth and **supplementary tasksheets** (labelled by an S) which are intended to help students with a relatively weak background in a particular topic. Commentaries for all the tasksheets are included in this unit guide.

The aim of the **exercises** is to check full understanding of principles and give the student confidence through reinforcement of his or her understanding.

Graphic calculators/microcomputers are used throughout the course. In particular, much use is made of graph plotters. The use of videos and equipment for practical work is also recommended.

As well as the textbooks and unit guides, there is a *Teacher's resource file*. This file contains: review sheets which may be used for homework or tests; datasheets; technology datasheets which give help with using particular calculators or pieces of software.

Introduction to the unit (for the teacher)

For many students, this is likely to be the final pure mathematics unit of their A level course. As such, it rounds off work on techniques of differentiation and integration as well as re-examining the basic idea of local straightness in a more algebraic manner.

The use of computers and graphic calculators is encouraged throughout the unit. In particular, the software packages *Real functions and graphs* and *Numerical solutions of equations* contain useful programs for parametric curve plotting and the Newton–Raphson method, respectively. There are technology datasheets to facilitate an equivalent use of graphic calculators.

Chapter 1

The idea of parametric equations is introduced through examples with natural parameters such as time or angle. Examples of parametric curves which are considered include circles and ellipses. The conversion of equations between Cartesian and parametric forms is used to introduce the further trigonometric ratios of sec, cosec and cot. The chapter concludes with a consideration of parametric differentiation and use of the chain rule.

Chapter 2

This chapter rounds off earlier work on techniques of algebraic differentiation. On completing this chapter, a student should be able to differentiate any elementary functions **and** any function formed from elementary functions by addition, subtraction, multiplication, division and/or composition. Finally, the techniques are extended to cases where the function is defined implicitly.

Chapter 3

The work of chapter 3 is introduced through examples based upon finding volumes. Whereas straightforward algorithms such as the chain rule and the product rule enable you to differentiate any function formed from combinations of elementary functions, the same is not true of integration. Techniques of integration, of use in various special cases, are studied in this chapter and in chapter 4.

Chapter 4

This chapter extends the work of chapter 3 and introduces the techniques of integration by parts and by substitution. Students should learn to recognise the various types of function for which these methods are appropriate. This chapter and the final two chapters of the unit can be studied in any order.

Chapter 5

The idea of the tangent approximation to a curve (Taylor's first approximation) leads into the powerful Newton–Raphson method for the solution of equations. For approximations centred on the value at $x = 0$, Taylor's first approximation generalises as Maclaurin's theorem.

Chapter 6

This final chapter introduces the need for a more algebraic approach to calculus. There is plenty of scope for high attaining students to investigate ideas from their previous study of calculus in a more rigorous way, based upon the use of differentiation from first principles.

Tasksheets and resources

This list gives an overview of where tasksheets are to be used.

1 Parameters

1.1 Curves which vary with time

The screen can be thought of as a Cartesian (x, y) plane with the origin at the bottom left-hand corner of the screen.

Suppose the spot moves so that, t seconds after it is at the origin, $x = 2t$ and $y = t$.

(a) Plot (or sketch) the positions of the spot after 1, 2, 3, 4 and 5 seconds.

(b) Explain why the line with Cartesian equation $y = \frac{1}{2}x$ will pass through your five points.

(c) How could you change the equations to make the spot follow the same path as before, but at twice the speed?

(d) Plot the graphs from (a) and (c) on a computer or graphic calculator screen, using a **parametric graph plotter**. (The technology datasheet, *Parametric curve plotting*, will help you.)

(a) If you tabulate the coordinates at one-second intervals, you obtain:

t	0	1	2	3	4	5
x	0	2	4	6	8	10
y	0	1	2	3	4	5

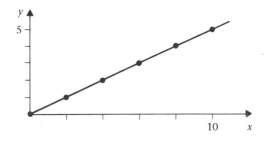

So the spot moves across the screen along the straight line $y = \frac{1}{2}x$.

(b) The equation $y = \frac{1}{2}x$ can be obtained by eliminating t from the equations:

$$x = 2t \quad \textcircled{1}$$
$$y = t \quad \textcircled{2}$$

From $\textcircled{1}$, $t = \frac{1}{2}x$
and so $y = t$
$$\Rightarrow y = \frac{1}{2}x$$

(c) $x = 4t$ and $y = 2t$

(d) –

1.4 Differentiating parametric equations

(a) For the circle given by the parametric equations:

$$x = 3\cos\theta, \quad y = 3\sin\theta$$

use the formula $\dfrac{dy}{dx} = \dfrac{dy}{d\theta} \div \dfrac{dx}{d\theta}$ to show that:

$$\frac{dy}{dx} = \frac{-\cos\theta}{\sin\theta}$$

(b) Check that this answer gives the correct values for the gradient of the circle when $\theta = 0$, $\frac{1}{2}\pi$ and π.

(a) $\dfrac{dy}{d\theta} = 3\cos\theta$ and $\dfrac{dx}{d\theta} = -3\sin\theta$

Then $\dfrac{dy}{dx} = \dfrac{3\cos\theta}{-3\sin\theta} = -\dfrac{\cos\theta}{\sin\theta}$

(b) At $\theta = 0$, $\dfrac{dy}{dx}$ is infinite.

At $\theta = \frac{1}{2}\pi$, $\dfrac{dy}{dx} = 0$

At $\theta = \pi$, $\dfrac{dy}{dx}$ is infinite.

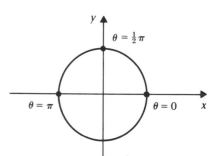

1.6 Velocity vectors

(a) Show on a graph that the points lie on a line.

(b) Find the Cartesian equation of this line.

(c) Find the velocity of the puck. Hence find its speed.

(d) Write expressions for x and y in terms of t. Differentiate these to find $\dot{x}$, i.e. $\dfrac{dx}{dt}$, and $\dot{y}$, i.e. $\dfrac{dy}{dt}$. What is the connection between these derivatives and the velocity, **v**, of the puck?

(e) Explain why both $\dfrac{dy}{dx}$ and $\dfrac{\dot{y}}{\dot{x}}$ represent the gradient of the line of points. What is the connection between the chain rule and the result:

$$\frac{dy}{dx} = \frac{\dot{y}}{\dot{x}}$$

(a)

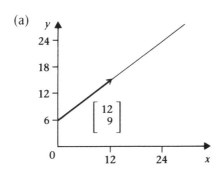

(b) $y = 0.75x + 6$

(c) The velocity is $\begin{bmatrix} 12 \\ 9 \end{bmatrix}\,\mathrm{m\,s^{-1}}$. The speed is $\sqrt{(12^2 + 9^2)} = 15\,\mathrm{m\,s^{-1}}$.

(d) $x = 12t$, $\quad y = 6 + 9t$

Differentiating, $\quad \dfrac{dx}{dt} = 12$ This is the rate at which the x-coordinate is increasing, a constant $12\,\mathrm{m\,s^{-1}}$ (the speed at which it is going **across** the pitch).

and $\quad \dfrac{dy}{dt} = 9$ This is the rate at which the y-coordinate is increasing, a constant $9\,\mathrm{m\,s^{-1}}$ (the speed at which it is going **up** the pitch).

3

These are the components of the velocity in the two directions and so:

$$\mathbf{v} = \begin{bmatrix} 12 \\ 9 \end{bmatrix} \mathrm{m\,s^{-1}}$$

In general:

$$\mathbf{v} = \begin{bmatrix} \dot{x} \\ \dot{y} \end{bmatrix}$$

(e) $\dfrac{dy}{dx}$ represents the gradient of the line of motion. This must

equal $\dfrac{\dot{y}}{\dot{x}}$, which represents the gradient of the velocity vector.

This result is generally true even if the motion is not in a straight line. It follows from the chain rule:

$$\frac{dy}{dt} = \frac{dy}{dx} \times \frac{dx}{dt} \quad \Rightarrow \quad \frac{dy}{dx} = \frac{dy}{dt} \div \frac{dx}{dt}$$

Ellipses

1 (a) $(3 \cos \theta, 3 \sin \theta)$

(b) $3 \sin \theta$

(c) $6 \cos \theta$

(d) $x = 6 \cos \theta$
$y = 3 \sin \theta$

(e) $R(0, 3)$
$Q(3, 0)$
$Q'(6, 0)$

(f) (i) $\pi \times 3^2 = 9\pi$

(ii) Since the curve is stretched by a factor 2 in the x direction, the area of the ellipse is $2 \times 9\pi = 18\pi$.

2 (a)

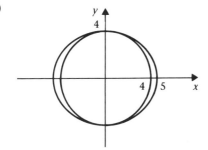

(b) The ellipse can be obtained from the circle by means of a one-way stretch, factor $\frac{5}{4}$ in the x direction.

(c) (i) 16π

(ii) $\frac{5}{4} \times 16\pi = 20\pi$

3 (a)

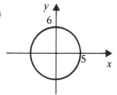

$x = 5 \cos \theta$
$y = 6 \sin \theta$

Major 10

minor 12

(b)

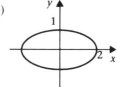

$x = 2 \cos \theta$
$y = \sin \theta$

4

2

(c)

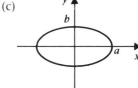

$x = a \cos \theta$
$y = b \sin \theta$

2a

2b

4 (a) $\qquad x = a \cos \theta, \quad y = b \sin \theta$

$$\Rightarrow \cos \theta = \frac{x}{a}, \quad \sin \theta = \frac{y}{b}$$

So, since $\cos^2 \theta + \sin^2 \theta = 1$, it follows that:

$$\left(\frac{x}{a}\right)^2 + \left(\frac{y}{b}\right)^2 = 1$$

or $\dfrac{x^2}{a^2} + \dfrac{y^2}{b^2} = 1,$ the Cartesian equation of the ellipse.

(b) Comparing with $\dfrac{x^2}{a^2} + \dfrac{y^2}{b^2} = 1,$

$a = 2, b = 3$

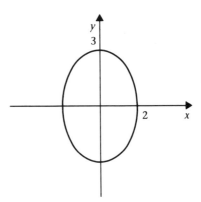

5 (a) The scale factors are: $\qquad a$ in the x direction,

$\qquad\qquad\qquad\qquad\qquad\qquad\quad b$ in the y direction.

(b) $\pi \times 1^2 = \pi$

Since the circle is stretched by a factor a, followed by b, the area of the ellipse is $\pi \times a \times b = \pi ab$.

Drawing parametric curves

1 (a)

θ	0	$\frac{1}{6}\pi$	$\frac{1}{4}\pi$	$\frac{1}{3}\pi$	$\frac{1}{2}\pi$
x	1	0.65	0.35	0.125	0
y	0	0.125	0.35	0.65	1

(b) As θ increases from $\frac{1}{2}\pi$ to π, the values of x become negative, but equal in magnitude to the values in the table. The values of y remain positive and equal to the values in the table, i.e. x decreases from 0 to -1 whilst y decreases from 1 to 0.

(c) For $\pi < \theta \le \frac{3}{2}\pi$ x and y are both negative, whilst for $\frac{3}{2}\pi < \theta \le 2\pi$, x is positive and y is negative.

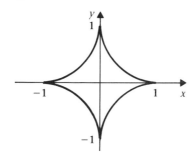

2

θ	0	$\frac{1}{6}\pi$	$\frac{1}{4}\pi$	$\frac{1}{3}\pi$	$\frac{1}{2}\pi$
x	0	0.02	0.08	0.18	0.57
y	0	0.13	0.29	0.5	1

As θ increases, x will continue to increase, though not steadily. y will oscillate between 0 and 2 (since $1 - \cos \pi = 1 - (-1) = 2$, after which $\cos \theta$ increases again).

The resulting curve is a **cycloid**, the path taken by a point on a moving circle.

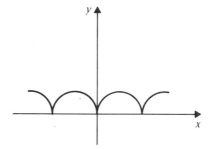

3 (a) $x = 0 \ \rightarrow \ t - -1, \quad y = \frac{1}{5}$
$y = 0 \ \Rightarrow \ t = -2, \quad x = -\frac{1}{4}$
i.e. the curve cuts the axes at $(0, \frac{1}{5})$ and $(-\frac{1}{4}, 0)$.

(b) As $t \rightarrow 2^-, \quad x \rightarrow +\infty, \quad y \rightarrow 2^-$ ($t \rightarrow 2^-$ means t approaches 2 from below.)
i.e. $y = 2$ is an asymptote.

(c) $t \rightarrow 4$ also yields an asymptote since it makes the denominator of y zero.
As $t \rightarrow 4^+, \quad x \rightarrow -\frac{5}{2}, \quad y \rightarrow -\infty$
$t \rightarrow 4^-, \quad x \rightarrow -\frac{5}{2}, \quad y \rightarrow +\infty$

(d) When $t = 0, \quad x = \frac{1}{2}, \quad y = \frac{1}{2}$ (It may be necessary to find a few more
points to increase your confidence.)

(e)

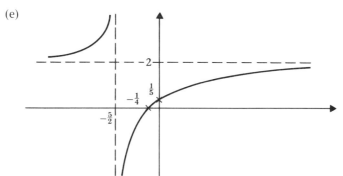

4 $x = 0 \ \Leftrightarrow \ t = 0 \ \Leftrightarrow \ y = 0$
As $t \rightarrow 1^+, \quad x \rightarrow -\infty, \quad y \rightarrow -\infty$
As $t \rightarrow 1^-, \quad x \rightarrow +\infty, \quad y \rightarrow +\infty$
As $t \rightarrow \infty, \quad x \rightarrow -2, \quad y \rightarrow -\infty$
As $t \rightarrow -\infty, \quad x \rightarrow -2, \quad y \rightarrow +\infty$

Again, plotting a few points will help.

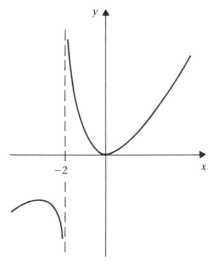

Trigonometric ratios

1 (a) $\sec \theta = \dfrac{c}{a}$ $\dfrac{1}{\cos \theta} = 1 \div \dfrac{a}{c} = \dfrac{c}{a}$

   (b) $\csc \theta = \dfrac{c}{b}$ $\dfrac{1}{\sin \theta} = 1 \div \dfrac{b}{c} = \dfrac{c}{b}$

   (c) $\cot \theta = \dfrac{a}{b}$ $\dfrac{1}{\tan \theta} = 1 \div \dfrac{b}{a} = \dfrac{a}{b}$

   (d) $\cot \theta = \dfrac{a}{b}$ $\dfrac{\cos \theta}{\sin \theta} = \dfrac{a}{c} \div \dfrac{b}{c} = \dfrac{a}{b}$

2

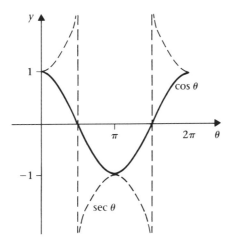

3 (a)

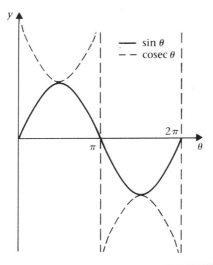

(b)

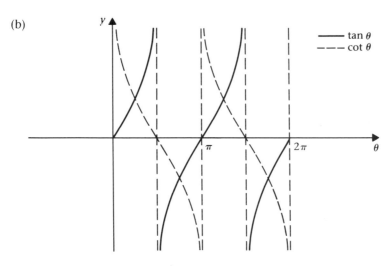

— tan θ
--- cot θ

4 The graphs of cot θ and cosec θ have negative gradients for $0 \leqslant \theta \leqslant \frac{1}{2}\pi$. So all the ratios starting with 'co' have this property.

5 (a) $\dfrac{\sin^2 \theta}{\cos^2 \theta} + \dfrac{\cos^2 \theta}{\cos^2 \theta} = \dfrac{1}{\cos^2 \theta}$

So, since $\dfrac{\sin \theta}{\cos \theta} = \tan \theta$ and $\dfrac{1}{\cos \theta} = \sec \theta$

$\tan^2 \theta + 1 = \sec^2 \theta$

(b) $\dfrac{\sin^2 \theta}{\sin^2 \theta} + \dfrac{\cos^2 \theta}{\sin^2 \theta} = \dfrac{1}{\sin^2 \theta}$

So, since $\dfrac{\cos \theta}{\sin \theta} = \cot \theta$ and $\dfrac{1}{\sin \theta} = \text{cosec } \theta$

$1 + \cot^2 \theta = \text{cosec}^2 \theta$

6 $\cot \theta = x$ and $\text{cosec } \theta = 2y$
So, using $1 + \cot^2 \theta = \text{cosec}^2 \theta$:

$$1 + x^2 = (2y)^2 \quad \text{or} \quad 4y^2 - x^2 = 1$$

2 Product rule

2.1 Combined functions

The diagrams below show three curves with their tangents at $x = 1$, $x = 1.5$ and $x = 2$ respectively.

In two cases you should be able to work out an algebraic expression for $\dfrac{dy}{dx}$ and so find the equation of the tangent. In the other case you will only be able to find the gradient of the tangent by a numerical method.

In which case must you use a numerical method? Think of some other functions for which you do not yet know how to work out a derivative. What sorts of function are they?

$e^x - 2 \sin x$ is the difference of two functions, both of which you know how to differentiate. The derivative is $e^x - 2 \cos x$.
$e^{\sin x}$ is a 'function of a function'. Its derivative is $\cos x \times e^{\sin x}$.

A numerical method will be needed to find the gradient of $y = x \sin x$.
As yet, you do not have an algebraic method for differentiating products.

2.5 Implicit differentiation

You can easily work out two of the three derivatives above, since you know that $\dfrac{d}{dx}(x^2) = 2x$ and $\dfrac{d}{dx}(9) = 0$.

(a) Let $z = y^2$. Use the chain rule, $\dfrac{dz}{dx} = \dfrac{dz}{dy} \times \dfrac{dy}{dx}$ to show that $\dfrac{d}{dx}(y^2) = 2y\dfrac{dy}{dx}$.

(b) Hence show that $\dfrac{dy}{dx} = -\dfrac{x}{y}$.

(c) Explain how the answer to (b) gives the expected values for the gradients of the tangents to the circle at the points $(0, 3)$, $(3, 0)$, $(0, -3)$ and $(-3, 0)$.

(a)
$$\frac{dz}{dy} = 2y$$

$$\Rightarrow \frac{dz}{dx} = \frac{dz}{dy} \times \frac{dy}{dx}$$

$$= 2y\frac{dy}{dx}$$

(b)
$$x^2 + y^2 = 9$$

$$\Rightarrow 2x + 2y\frac{dy}{dx} = 0$$

$$\Rightarrow \frac{dy}{dx} = -\frac{2x}{2y} = -\frac{x}{y}$$

(c) The gradient should be zero at $(0, 3)$ and $(0, -3)$.
The gradient should be infinite at $(3, 0)$ and $(-3, 0)$.

It is easy to see that this is the case by substituting the appropriate values for x and y into the equation:

$$\frac{dy}{dx} = -\frac{x}{y}$$

Products

1 (a) $\dfrac{dy}{dx} = 2x \sin x + x^2 \cos x$

$= 2.22$ at $x = 1$

(b) –

2 (a) $\dfrac{dy}{dx} = -\frac{1}{2} \sin (\frac{1}{2}x) \times (4x - \frac{1}{2}x^2) + \cos (\frac{1}{2}x) \times (4 - x)$

$= (\frac{1}{4}x^2 - 2x) \sin (\frac{1}{2}x) + (4 - x) \cos (\frac{1}{2}x)$

(b) –

3 Whatever functions you choose, you should find that the product rule gives correct gradient functions.

4 (a) $\dfrac{d}{dx} (x^3 \times x^2) = 3x^2 \times x^2 + x^3 \times 2x$

$= 3x^4 + 2x^4$

$= 5x^4$ as expected.

(b) –

(c) $\dfrac{d}{dx} (x^a \times x^b) = ax^{a-1} \times x^b + x^a \times bx^{b-1}$

$= ax^{a+b-1} + bx^{a+b-1}$

$= (a + b) x^{a+b-1}$ as expected

Quotients

This tasksheet shows how to derive the quotient rule from the product rule.

1 $\dfrac{dy}{dx} = (\sin x)^{-1} - x\cos x\,(\sin x)^{-2}$

$\quad = \dfrac{1}{\sin x} - \dfrac{x\cos x}{\sin^2 x}$

$\quad = \dfrac{\sin x - x\cos x}{\sin^2 x}$

2 (a) The derivative is:

$$e^x(\sin x)^{-1} - e^x\cos x(\sin x)^{-2} \quad \text{or} \quad \dfrac{e^x}{\sin x} - \dfrac{e^x\cos x}{\sin^2 x}$$

This is equal to:

$$\dfrac{e^x\sin x - e^x\cos x}{\sin^2 x}$$

which is the expression obtained by using formula ①.

(b) –

3 By the chain rule:

$$\dfrac{d(v^{-1})}{dx} = -1\,v^{-2}\,\dfrac{dv}{dx}$$

So $\dfrac{dy}{dx} = v^{-1}\dfrac{du}{dx} - uv^{-2}\dfrac{dv}{dx}$

$\quad = \dfrac{1}{v}\dfrac{du}{dx} - \dfrac{u}{v^2}\dfrac{dv}{dx}$

$\quad = \dfrac{v\dfrac{du}{dx} - u\dfrac{dv}{dx}}{v^2}$

Differentiation practice

1 By the chain rule: $\dfrac{dy}{dx} = 2\sin x \cos x$ (or $\sin 2x$)

2 By the chain rule: $\dfrac{dy}{dx} = -12\sin 4x$

3 $y = \dfrac{1}{x^2}$ or x^{-2} $\dfrac{dy}{dx} = -2x^{-3}$ or $\dfrac{-2}{x^3}$

4 By the chain rule: $y = (2x+5)^{-1}$

$\dfrac{dy}{dx} = -2(2x+5)^{-2}$ or $\dfrac{-2}{(2x+5)^2}$

5 Using parametric differentiation: $\dfrac{dy}{dx} = \dfrac{6}{2t}$ or $\dfrac{3}{t}$

6 Using the product rule and the chain rule: $\dfrac{dy}{dx} = 2e^{2x}\sin\tfrac{1}{2}x + \tfrac{1}{2}e^{2x}\cos\tfrac{1}{2}x$

$\dfrac{dy}{dx} = e^{2x}(2\sin\tfrac{1}{2}x + \tfrac{1}{2}\cos\tfrac{1}{2}x)$

7 By the chain rule: $\dfrac{dy}{dx} = 12x(2x^2-3)^2$

8 By the chain rule: $\dfrac{dy}{dx} = 4\left(\dfrac{1}{4x}\right) = \dfrac{1}{x}$

Or: $y = \ln 4x = \ln 4 + \ln x.$ So $\dfrac{dy}{dx} = \dfrac{1}{x}$

9 By implicit differentiation: $2xy + x^2\dfrac{dy}{dx} = 0,$ so $\dfrac{dy}{dx} = \dfrac{-2xy}{x^2} = \dfrac{-2y}{x}$

Or: $y = \dfrac{36}{x^2} = 36x^{-2};$ $\dfrac{dy}{dx} = -72x^{-3} = \dfrac{-72}{x^3}$

10 By parametric differentiation: $\dfrac{dy}{dx} = \dfrac{3\cos\theta}{-4\sin\theta}$ or $-0.75\cot\theta$

11 Using the product rule and the chain rule: $\dfrac{dy}{dx} = (2x-3)^4 + 8x(2x-3)^3$

12 $y = x^4(2x - 3) = 2x^5 - 3x^4$

$$\frac{dy}{dx} = 10x^4 - 12x^3$$

13 By parametric differentiation: $\dfrac{dy}{dx} = \dfrac{-6 \sin 3\theta}{2 \cos 2\theta} = \dfrac{-3 \sin 3\theta}{\cos 2\theta}$

14 By implicit differentiation: $2x + 2y \dfrac{dy}{dx} = 0$

$$\frac{dy}{dx} = \frac{-x}{y}$$

15 By the chain rule: $y = (5x)^{\frac{1}{2}}$

$$\frac{dy}{dx} = (\tfrac{1}{2} \times 5)(5x)^{-\frac{1}{2}} \quad \text{or} \quad \frac{2.5}{\sqrt{(5x)}}$$

16 By parametric differentiation: $\dfrac{dy}{dx} = 3t^2 \div -\dfrac{1}{t^2} \quad \text{or} \quad -3t^4$

17 By implicit differentiation: $2x + 3y + 3x \dfrac{dy}{dx} + 4y \dfrac{dy}{dx} = 0$

$$\frac{dy}{dx} = \frac{-(2x + 3y)}{(3x + 4y)}$$

18 By the quotient rule: $\dfrac{dy}{dx} = \dfrac{\cos 2x \cos x + 2 \sin x \sin 2x}{\cos^2 2x}$

19 By implicit differentiation: $3e^{3x}y + e^{3x} \dfrac{dy}{dx} = 2x$

$$\frac{dy}{dx} = \frac{(2x - 3ye^{3x})}{e^{3x}}$$

Or: $y = \dfrac{x^2}{e^{3x}}$ and use the quotient rule:

$$\frac{dy}{dx} = \frac{2xe^{3x} - 3x^2e^{3x}}{(e^{3x})^2} = \frac{2x - 3x^2}{e^{3x}}$$

20 $y = 12 - x^2$, so $\dfrac{dy}{dx} = -2x$

3 Volume

3.1 Containers

Not all industrial containers are quite so simple. Calculate the volume of each of these containers and make a rough sketch of what you think the (h, V) graph will look like.

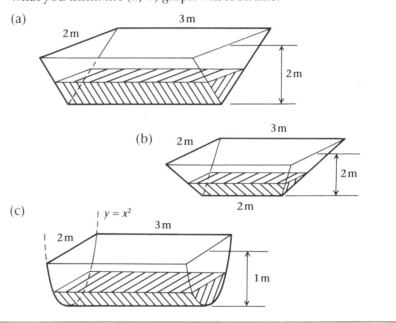

(a)

2m

3m

2m

(b)

2m

3m

2m

2m

(c)

$y = x^2$

2m

3m

1m

(a) This is a simple prism of length 3 m and cross-sectional area 2 m². Its volume is 6 m³ and the (h, V) graph will be as shown.

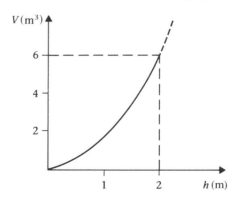

(b) The volume of the container will equal the sum of the volumes of the triangular prism and the rectangular based pyramid shown below.

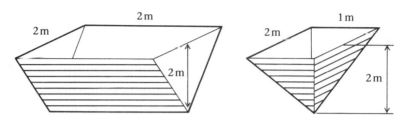

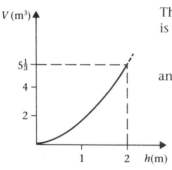

The volume of the container is therefore:

$$\tfrac{1}{2} \times 2 \times 2 \times 2 + \tfrac{1}{3} \times 2 \times 1 \times 2 = 5\tfrac{1}{3}\,\text{m}^3$$

and the (h, V) graph will be as shown.

(c) This container is also a prism. However, calculating the cross-sectional area is a little more difficult than in part (a).

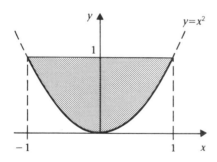

The cross-sectional area is:

$$2 - \int_{-1}^{1} x^2\,\mathrm{d}x = 2 - \left[\tfrac{1}{3}x^3\right]_{-1}^{1}$$

$$= 1\tfrac{1}{3}\,\text{m}^2$$

The volume of the container is $3 \times 1\tfrac{1}{3} = 4\,\text{m}^3$.

The (h, V) graph is as shown.

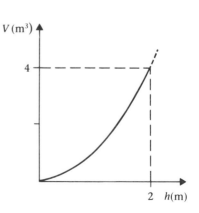

3.2 Volumes of revolution

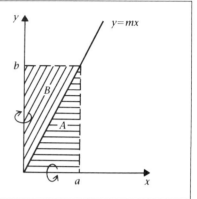

The two shaded areas shown on the graph are equal.

Would you expect the volume generated by rotating area A about the x-axis to be the same as that obtained by rotating B about the y-axis?

Justify your answer.

Many people would expect the two volumes to be equal. It is easy to prove otherwise. Both volumes formed will be cones.

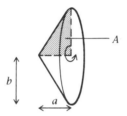

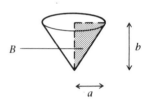

The volume of a cone is given by the formula $V = \frac{1}{3}\pi r^2 h$.

The two cones formed will have volumes $\frac{1}{3}\pi b^2 a$ for area A and $\frac{1}{3}\pi a^2 b$ for area B. These volumes will only be equal if $a = b$.

You could have calculated the volumes formed using the technique developed in the tasksheet. The volume formed by rotating area A about the x-axis is:

$$\int_0^a \pi y^2 \, dx = \int_0^a \pi m^2 x^2 \, dx$$

$$= \left[\frac{1}{3}\pi m^2 x^3 \right]_0^a$$

$$= \frac{1}{3}\pi m^2 a^3$$

$$= \frac{1}{3}\pi b^2 a \qquad \text{because } m^2 a^2 = b^2$$

This confirms the formula for the volume of a cone.

3.3 Integration by inspection

> Discuss what functions you might try to differentiate to solve
> the following integrals.
>
> (a) $\displaystyle\int x \cos x^2 \, dx$ (b) $\displaystyle\int x \cos 2x \, dx$
>
> (c) $\displaystyle\int \cos 2x \, dx$ (d) $\displaystyle\int \cos x^2 \, dx$

(a) Differentiating the function $\sin x^2$ seems to be a sensible starting
point.

$$\frac{d}{dx}(\sin x^2) = 2x \cos x^2 \quad \text{using the chain rule}$$

so $\displaystyle\int x \cos x^2 \, dx = \tfrac{1}{2} \sin x^2 + c$

(b) Differentiating the function $x \sin 2x$ by the product rule,

$$\Rightarrow \quad \frac{d}{dx}(x \sin 2x) \quad = 2x \cos 2x + \sin 2x$$

$$\Rightarrow \qquad x \sin 2x \quad = 2\int x \cos 2x \, dx + \int \sin 2x \, dx$$

$$\Rightarrow \quad 2\int x \cos 2x \, dx = x \sin 2x - \int \sin 2x \, dx$$

$$\Rightarrow \quad 2\int x \cos 2x \, dx = x \sin 2x + \tfrac{1}{2} \cos 2x + c$$

$$\Rightarrow \quad \int x \cos 2x \, dx \quad = \tfrac{1}{2}x \sin 2x + \tfrac{1}{4} \cos 2x + c$$

(c) Differentiating the function $\sin 2x$ by inspection,

$$\Rightarrow \quad \frac{d}{dx}(\sin 2x) = 2 \cos 2x$$

so $\displaystyle\int \cos 2x \, dx = \tfrac{1}{2} \sin 2x$

(d) It is not possible to find an algebraic solution to $\displaystyle\int \cos x^2 \, dx$.

3.4 Integrating trigonometric functions

> (a) Use the addition formulas to show that $\sin\left(\frac{1}{2}\pi - \theta\right) = \cos\theta$. Obtain similar results for $\cos\left(\frac{1}{2}\pi - \theta\right)$, $\sec\left(\frac{1}{2}\pi - \theta\right)$ and $\tan\left(\frac{1}{2}\pi - \theta\right)$.
>
> (b) Show how you can use the addition formulas to prove the **sum and difference formulas**.

(a) $\sin\left(\frac{1}{2}\pi - \theta\right) = \sin\frac{1}{2}\pi\cos\theta - \cos\frac{1}{2}\pi\sin\theta = \cos\theta$
$\cos\left(\frac{1}{2}\pi - \theta\right) = \sin\theta$

$\sec\left(\frac{1}{2}\pi - \theta\right) = \dfrac{1}{\cos\left(\frac{1}{2}\pi - \theta\right)} = \dfrac{1}{\sin\theta} = \operatorname{cosec}\theta$

$\tan\left(\frac{1}{2}\pi - \theta\right) = \dfrac{\sin\left(\frac{1}{2}\pi - \theta\right)}{\cos\left(\frac{1}{2}\pi - \theta\right)} = \dfrac{\cos\theta}{\sin\theta} = \cot\theta$

You may have wondered about the significance of the prefix 'co' in the names of trigonometric functions. It comes from **complementary** angles, which are angles whose sum is 90° (or $\frac{1}{2}\pi$ radians).

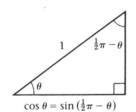

$\cos\theta = \sin\left(\frac{1}{2}\pi - \theta\right)$

The diagram shows that, when θ is acute,

$$\cos\theta = \sin\left(\frac{1}{2}\pi - \theta\right)$$

The **co**sine of an angle is the sine of the **co**mplementary angle.

(b)
$$\cos (A + B) = \cos A\cos B - \sin A\sin B$$
$$\cos (A - B) = \cos A\cos B + \sin A\sin B +$$

$$\cos (A + B) + \cos (A - B) = 2\cos A\cos B$$

$$-\cos (A + B) = -\cos A\cos B + \sin A\sin B$$
$$\cos (A - B) = \cos A\cos B + \sin A\sin B +$$

$$-\cos (A + B) + \cos (A - B) = \qquad 2\sin A\sin B$$

$$\sin (A + B) = \sin A\cos B + \cos A\sin B$$
$$\sin (A - B) = \sin A\cos B - \cos A\sin B +$$

$$\sin (A + B) + \sin (A - B) = 2\sin A\cos B$$

21

Thin slabs

1 (a) The volume of the container at height h is given by the equation $V = 4h^{1.5}$. The container will be a quarter full when $V = 1\,\mathrm{m}^3$.

$$4h^{1.5} = 1 \;\Rightarrow\; h = (\tfrac{1}{4})^{\frac{2}{3}}$$
$$= 0.3968\ldots\mathrm{m}$$

The container will be a quarter full when $h \approx 40\,\mathrm{cm}$.

(b) The volume when the container is half full is $2\,\mathrm{m}^3$.

$$4h^{1.5} = 2 \;\Rightarrow\; h = (\tfrac{1}{2})^{\frac{2}{3}}$$
$$= 0.6299\ldots\mathrm{m}$$

The container will be half full when $h \approx 63\,\mathrm{cm}$.

(c) The container will be three-quarters full when $h \approx 83\,\mathrm{cm}$.

2 The width, w, of the slab increases uniformly from 0 to 2 as the height, h, increases from 0 to 2. So $w = h$.

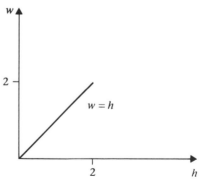

The length, l, of the slab increases uniformly from 2 to 3 as the height, h, increases from 0 to 2. So $l = 2 + \tfrac{1}{2}h$.

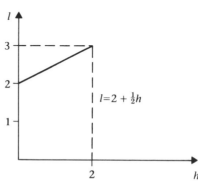

3   The volume of a slab at height h is $h(2 + \frac{1}{2}h)$ dh. Hence, the volume of the container is:

$$V = \int_0^2 h(2 + \tfrac{1}{2}h)\, \mathrm{d}h$$

$$= \int_0^2 2h + \tfrac{1}{2}h^2\, \mathrm{d}h$$

$$= \left[h^2 + \tfrac{1}{6}h^3 \right]_0^2$$

$$= 5\tfrac{1}{3}\,\mathrm{m}^3$$

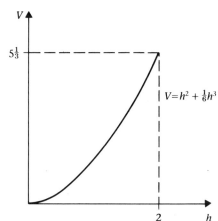

4   The container is half full when $V = 2\frac{2}{3}$.

$$h^2 + \tfrac{1}{6}h^3 = 2\tfrac{2}{3} \;\Rightarrow\; h \approx 1.46\,\mathrm{m}$$

The equation can be solved by decimal search, using the Newton–Raphson method, or by plotting the graph and reading off the solution.

5   The increase in volume is $\left[h^2 + \tfrac{1}{6}h^3 \right]_{1.1}^{1.4} = 0.9855\,\mathrm{m}^3$.

Volumes

1 (a) If the rectangle of height y and width dx is rotated completely about the x-axis, it describes a cylinder of radius y and width dx and hence will have volume $\pi y^2\, dx$.

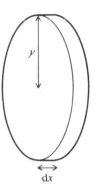

(b) If $y = x^2$, $y^2 = (x^2)^2 = x^4$

(c) Volume $= \displaystyle\int_0^2 \pi y^2\, dx = \int_0^2 \pi x^4\, dx = \left[\tfrac{1}{5}\pi x^5 \right]_0^2 = \tfrac{1}{5}\pi 2^5 - \tfrac{1}{5}\pi 0^5 = \tfrac{32}{5}\pi$

2 (a) Volume $= \displaystyle\int_0^2 \pi y^2\, dx = \int_0^2 \pi(x^2 + 1)^2\, dx = \int_0^2 \pi(x^4 + 2x^2 + 1)\, dx$

$= \left[\pi(\tfrac{1}{5}x^5 + \tfrac{2}{3}x^3 + x) \right]_0^2 = 13\,\tfrac{11}{15}\pi$

(b) The graph $y = x^2 - 2x$ cuts the x-axis where $x^2 - 2x = 0$
$\Rightarrow x(x - 2) = 0 \Rightarrow x = 0$ or $x = 2$

Volume $= \displaystyle\int_0^2 \pi y^2\, dx = \int_0^2 \pi(x^4 - 4x^3 + 4x^2)\, dx$

$= \left[\pi(\tfrac{1}{5}x^5 - x^4 + \tfrac{4}{3}x^3) \right]_0^2$

$= \tfrac{16}{15}\pi$

3 When a rectangle, of length x and height dy, is rotated about the y-axis, it describes a cylinder of volume $\pi x^2\, dy$. It follows that the volume of the solid obtained by rotating the area about the y-axis

$= \displaystyle\int_0^4 \pi x^2\, dy$

$= \displaystyle\int_0^4 \pi y\, dy = \left[\pi \tfrac{1}{2}y^2 \right]_0^4 = 8\pi$

4 $y = \dfrac{1}{x} \Rightarrow x = \dfrac{1}{y}$

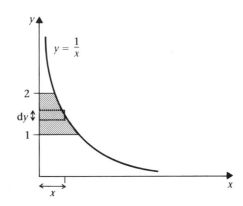

Volume $= \displaystyle\int_1^2 \pi x^2 \, \mathrm{d}y = \int_1^2 \pi \, \dfrac{1}{y^2} \, \mathrm{d}y$

$\qquad\quad = \tfrac{1}{2}\pi$

5 The gradient of the join of $(4, 3)$ to $(6, 5)$ $= \dfrac{5 - 3}{6 - 4} = 1.$

The equation of this join is $\qquad y - 3 = 1(x - 4) \Rightarrow x = y + 1.$
The volume obtained by rotating the area bounded by this line segment, $y = 3$, $y = 5$

and the y-axis about the y-axis is $\displaystyle\int_3^5 \pi x^2 \, \mathrm{d}y = \int_3^5 \pi(y^2 + 2y + 1) \, \mathrm{d}y$

$\qquad\qquad\qquad\qquad\qquad\qquad\qquad\quad = 50\tfrac{2}{3}\pi$

The equation of the circle is $x^2 + y^2 = 25 \Rightarrow x^2 = 25 - y^2.$
The volume obtained by rotating the area bounded by the arc of the circle, $y = 3$ and

both x- and y-axes about the y-axis is $\displaystyle\int_0^3 \pi x^2 \, \mathrm{d}y = \int_0^3 \pi(25 - y^2) \, \mathrm{d}y$

$\qquad\qquad\qquad\qquad\qquad\qquad = 66\pi$

The gradient of the join of $(4, -2)$ to $(5, 0)$ is $\dfrac{0 - (-2)}{5 - 4} = 2.$

The equation of this join is $y - 0 = 2(x - 5) \Rightarrow x = \tfrac{1}{2}y + 5.$
The volume obtained by rotating the area bounded by this line segment, $y = -2$ and

the x- and y-axes about the y-axis is $\displaystyle\int_{-2}^0 \pi x^2 \, \mathrm{d}y = \int_{-2}^0 \pi(\tfrac{1}{4}y^2 + 5y + 25) \, \mathrm{d}y$

$\qquad\qquad\qquad\qquad\qquad\qquad = 40\tfrac{2}{3}\pi$

The volume of the vase is $50\tfrac{2}{3}\pi + 66\pi + 40\tfrac{2}{3}\pi = 157\tfrac{1}{3}\pi.$

4 Integration techniques

4.1 Integration by parts

(a) What happens if, in the example above, you let
$$u = \cos 2x \quad \text{and} \quad \frac{dv}{dx} = x?$$

(b) What happens if you use integration by parts to find
$$\int x \cos x^2 \, dx?$$

(a) $u = \cos 2x \Rightarrow \dfrac{du}{dx} = -2 \sin 2x \quad \text{and} \quad \dfrac{dv}{dx} = x \Rightarrow v = \tfrac{1}{2}x^2$

$$\Rightarrow \int x \cos 2x \, dx = \tfrac{1}{2}x^2 \cos 2x + \int x^2 \sin 2x \, dx$$

This rearrangement of the integral does not make it simpler to evaluate. If you make the wrong choice as to which part of the product should be u and which should be $\dfrac{dv}{dx}$, then you will generally find that the integral has become more, rather than less, complicated. Experience will enable you to spot which part of the product to integrate and which to differentiate.

(b) If you let $u = x$ and $\dfrac{dv}{dx} = \cos x^2$, then $\dfrac{du}{dx} = 1$ looks promising.

However, $\dfrac{dv}{dx} = \cos x^2$ has no algebraic solution and so the integral cannot be rearranged using the technique of integration by parts.

If you let $u = \cos x^2$ and $\dfrac{dv}{dx} = x$, then $\dfrac{du}{dx} = -2x \sin x^2$ and $v = \tfrac{1}{2}x^2$.

The resulting rearrangement becomes:

$$\int x \cos x^2 \, dx = \tfrac{1}{2}x^2 \cos x^2 + \int x^3 \sin x^2 \, dx$$

which does not help you.

In fact, this integral can be evaluated by inspection.

$$\int x \cos x^2 \, dx = \tfrac{1}{2} \sin x^2 + c$$

which makes the point that integration by parts will not necessarily be a sensible method to choose just because an integral **can** be written as the product of two functions.

4.2 Integration by substitution

> Discuss how you would find the integral of:
>
> (a) $x(x^2 + 3)^4$ (b) $x^3(x^2 + 3)^4$ (c) $(x^2 + 3)^4$

(a) To evaluate $\int x(x^2 + 3)^4 \, dx$, you could:

- multiply out the bracket;
- try the substitution $u = x^2 + 3$;
- try integration by parts;
- integrate by inspection.

Integration by inspection is the most sensible method.

$$\frac{d}{dx}\left((x^2 + 3)^5\right) = 10x(x^2 + 3)^4 \;\Rightarrow\; \int x(x^2 + 3)^4 \, dx = \tfrac{1}{10}(x^2 + 3)^5 + c$$

Multiplying out the bracket would be tedious and substitution is unnecessarily complicated. Integration by parts would not be a sensible method for this integral.

(b) To evaluate $\int x^3(x^2 + 3)^4 \, dx$, you could:

- multiply out the bracket;
- try the substitution $u = x^2 + 3$;
- try integration by parts;
- integrate by inspection.

Multiplying out the bracket would again be tedious. Neither integration by parts nor by inspection are sensible methods.

$$\text{Let } u = x^2 + 3 \;\Rightarrow\; \frac{du}{dx} = 2x \quad \text{and} \quad \frac{dx}{du} = \frac{1}{2x}$$

$$\Rightarrow \int x^3(x^2 + 3)^4 \, dx = \int \tfrac{1}{2}x^2(x^2 + 3)^4 \, du$$

$$= \tfrac{1}{2} \int (u - 3)u^4 \, du$$

$$= \tfrac{1}{2} \int (u^5 - 3u^4) \, du$$

$$= \tfrac{1}{2}(\tfrac{1}{6}u^6 - \tfrac{3}{5}u^5) + c$$

$$= \tfrac{1}{12}(x^2 + 3)^6 - \tfrac{3}{10}(x^2 + 3)^5 + c$$

(c) To evaluate $\displaystyle\int (x^2 + 3)^4 \, dx$, you could:

- multiply out the bracket;
- try the substitution $u = x^2 + 3$;
- try integration by parts;
- integrate by inspection.

Neither integration by parts nor by inspection are sensible methods. Multiplying out the bracket would again be tedious, so you might try substitution.

$$\text{Let } u = x^2 + 3 \;\Rightarrow\; \frac{du}{dx} = 2x \quad \text{and} \quad \frac{dx}{du} = \frac{1}{2x}$$

$$\Rightarrow \int (x^2 + 3)^4 \, dx = \int (x^2 + 3)^4 \, \frac{1}{2x} \, du$$

$$= \int \frac{u^4}{2\sqrt{(u - 3)}} \, du$$

This has not simplified the integral, so you are left with the option of multiplying out the bracket.

$$\int (x^2 + 3)^4 \, dx = \int x^8 + 12x^6 + 54x^4 + 108x^2 + 81 \, dx$$

$$= \tfrac{1}{9}x^9 + \tfrac{12}{7}x^7 + \tfrac{54}{5}x^5 + \tfrac{108}{3}x^3 + 81x + c$$

4.3 The reciprocal function

(a) Explain why $\displaystyle\int_{-b}^{-a}\frac{1}{x}\,dx \neq \left[\ln x\right]_{-b}^{-a} = \ln(-a) - \ln(-b)$

(b) By symmetry, $\displaystyle\int_{-b}^{-a}\frac{1}{x}\,dx = -\int_{a}^{b}\frac{1}{x}\,dx$. Use this to

express $\displaystyle\int_{-b}^{-a}\frac{1}{x}\,dx$ in terms of $\ln a$ and $\ln b$.

(c) Explain why $\displaystyle\int_{-b}^{-a}\frac{1}{x}\,dx = \left[\ln|x|\right]_{-b}^{-a}$

(a) The function $y = \ln x$ is not defined for $x \leqslant 0$.

(b) $\displaystyle\int_{-b}^{-a}\frac{1}{x}\,dx = -\int_{a}^{b}\frac{1}{x}\,dx = -\left[\ln x\right]_{a}^{b} = \ln a - \ln b$

(c) $\displaystyle\int_{-b}^{-a}\frac{1}{x}\,dx = \ln a - \ln b$

$$= \ln|-a| - \ln|-b|$$

$$= \left[\ln|x|\right]_{-b}^{-a}$$

where the symbol $|x|$ denotes the absolute (or positive) value of x. For example, $|-3.5| = |3.5| = 3.5$.

29

4.4 Partial fractions

Evaluate $\displaystyle\int_1^2 \frac{5}{(x-3)(x+2)}\,dx$ using a numerical method

and $\displaystyle\int_1^2 \frac{1}{x-3} - \frac{1}{x+2}\,dx$ by algebra.

Explain why the two integrals have the same answer.

Using the mid-ordinate rule with 100 strips:

$$\int_1^2 \frac{5}{(x-3)(x+2)}\,dx \approx -0.9808 \qquad \text{(to 4 d.p.)}$$

$$\int_1^2 \frac{1}{x-3} - \frac{1}{x+2}\,dx = \Big[\ln|x-3| - \ln|x+2|\Big]_1^2$$

$$= \ln(1) - \ln(4) - \ln(2) + \ln(3)$$

$$= \ln(\tfrac{3}{8}) = -0.980829253 \qquad \text{(to 9 d.p.)}$$

You would expect the same answers as the two integrals are simply two different ways of writing the same integral. The two functions are equal because:

$$\frac{1}{x-3} - \frac{1}{x+2} = \frac{(x+2)}{(x-3)(x+2)} - \frac{(x-3)}{(x-3)(x+2)}$$

$$= \frac{(x+2) - (x-3)}{(x-3)(x+2)}$$

$$= \frac{5}{(x-3)(x+2)}$$

By parts

1 $I = e^x \sin x - \displaystyle\int e^x \sin x \, dx$

$I = e^x \sin x - \left[-e^x \cos x + \displaystyle\int e^x \cos x \, dx \right]$

$I = e^x \sin x + e^x \cos x - I$

$2I = e^x \sin x + e^x \cos x$

$I = \frac{1}{2} e^x (\sin x + \cos x)$

2 $u = \cos x \Rightarrow \dfrac{du}{dx} = -\sin x$ and $\dfrac{dv}{dx} = e^x \Rightarrow v = e^x$

$I = \displaystyle\int e^x \cos x \, dx = \cos x \times e^x - \int -\sin x \times e^x \, dx$

For $\displaystyle\int \sin x \times e^x \, dx$, let $u = \sin x \Rightarrow \dfrac{du}{dx} = \cos x$ and $\dfrac{dv}{dx} = e^x \Rightarrow v = e^x$

$\displaystyle\int \sin x \times e^x \, dx = \sin x \times e^x - \int \cos x \times e^x \, dx + c$

$\Rightarrow I = e^x \cos x + e^x \sin x - I + c$

$\Rightarrow 2I = e^x \cos x + e^x \sin x + c$

$\Rightarrow I = \frac{1}{2}(e^x \cos x + e^x \sin x) + K$ (where $K = \frac{1}{2}c$)

In this case, the choice of u and $\dfrac{dv}{dx}$ does not matter.

3 (a) $u = e^x \Rightarrow \dfrac{du}{dx} = e^x$ and $\dfrac{dv}{dx} = \sin x \Rightarrow v = -\cos x$

$I = \displaystyle\int e^x \sin x \, dx = -e^x \cos x + \int e^x \cos x \, dx$

For $\displaystyle\int e^x \cos x \, dx$, let $u = e^x \Rightarrow \dfrac{du}{dx} = e^x$ and $\dfrac{dv}{dx} = \cos x \Rightarrow v = \sin x$

$\displaystyle\int e^x \cos x \, dx = e^x \sin x - \int e^x \sin x \, dx + c$

$\Rightarrow I = -e^x \cos x + e^x \sin x - I + c$

$\Rightarrow 2I = e^x \sin x - e^x \cos x + c$

$\Rightarrow I = \frac{1}{2}(e^x \sin x - e^x \cos x) + K$ (where $K = \frac{1}{2}c$)

(b) Put $u = e^{2x} \Rightarrow \dfrac{du}{dx} = 2e^{2x}$ and $\dfrac{dv}{dx} = \cos x \Rightarrow v = \sin x$

$$I = \int e^{2x} \cos x \, dx = e^{2x} \sin x - \int 2e^{2x} \sin x \, dx$$

For $\displaystyle\int 2e^{2x} \sin x \, dx$, let $u = 2e^{2x} \Rightarrow \dfrac{du}{dx} = 4e^{2x}$ and $\dfrac{dv}{dx} = \sin x \Rightarrow v = -\cos x$

$$\int 2e^{2x} \sin x \, dx = 2e^{2x}(-\cos x) - \int 4e^{2x}(-\cos x) \, dx + c$$

$\Rightarrow I = e^{2x} \sin x + 2e^{2x} \cos x - 4I + c$
$\Rightarrow 5I = e^{2x} \sin x + 2e^{2x} \cos x + c$
$\Rightarrow I = \frac{1}{5}(e^{2x} \sin x + 2e^{2x} \cos x) + K$ (where $K = \frac{1}{5}c$)

(c) $u = e^x \Rightarrow \dfrac{du}{dx} = e^x$ and $\dfrac{dv}{dx} = \sin 2x \Rightarrow v = -\frac{1}{2} \cos 2x$

$$I = \int e^x \sin 2x \, dx = e^x(-\tfrac{1}{2} \cos 2x) - \int e^x(-\tfrac{1}{2} \cos 2x) \, dx$$

For $\displaystyle\int \tfrac{1}{2} e^x \cos 2x \, dx$, let $u = \tfrac{1}{2}e^x \Rightarrow \dfrac{du}{dx} = \tfrac{1}{2}e^x$ and $\dfrac{dv}{dx} = \cos 2x \Rightarrow v = \tfrac{1}{2} \sin 2x$

$$\int \tfrac{1}{2}e^x \cos 2x \, dx = \tfrac{1}{2}e^x \times \tfrac{1}{2} \sin 2x - \int \tfrac{1}{2}e^x \times \tfrac{1}{2} \sin 2x + c$$

$\Rightarrow I \;\; = -\frac{1}{2}e^x \cos 2x + \frac{1}{4} e^x \sin 2x - \frac{1}{4}I + c$
$\Rightarrow \frac{5}{4}I = -\frac{1}{2}e^x \cos 2x + \frac{1}{4}e^x \sin 2x + c$
$\Rightarrow I \;\; = -\frac{1}{5}(2e^x \cos 2x - e^x \sin 2x) + K$ (where $K = \frac{4}{5}c$)

(d) $u = e^{0.5x} \Rightarrow \dfrac{du}{dx} = \tfrac{1}{2}e^{0.5x}$ and $\dfrac{dv}{dx} = \cos 2x \Rightarrow v = \tfrac{1}{2} \sin 2x$

$$I = \int e^{0.5x} \cos 2x \, dx = e^{0.5x} (\tfrac{1}{2} \sin 2x) - \int \tfrac{1}{2} e^{0.5x} (\tfrac{1}{2} \sin 2x) \, dx$$

For $\displaystyle\int \tfrac{1}{4} e^{0.5x} \sin 2x \, dx$, let $u = \tfrac{1}{4}e^{0.5x}$ and $v = -\tfrac{1}{2}\cos 2x$

$$\int \tfrac{1}{4}e^{0.5x} \sin 2x \, dx = \tfrac{1}{4}e^{0.5x} (-\tfrac{1}{2} \cos 2x) - \int \tfrac{1}{8} e^{0.5x} (-\tfrac{1}{2} \cos 2x) \, dx + c$$

$\Rightarrow I = \frac{1}{2}e^{0.5x} \sin 2x + \frac{1}{8}e^{0.5x} \cos 2x - \frac{1}{16}I + c$
$\frac{17}{16}I = \frac{1}{2}e^{0.5x} \sin 2x + \frac{1}{8}e^{0.5x} \cos 2x + c$
$\Rightarrow I = \frac{1}{17}(8e^{0.5x} \sin 2x + 2e^{0.5x} \cos 2x) + K$ (where $K = \frac{16}{17} c$)

4 (a) Put $u = \sin x \implies \dfrac{\mathrm{d}u}{\mathrm{d}x} = \cos x$ and $\dfrac{\mathrm{d}v}{\mathrm{d}x} = \cos x \implies v = \sin x$

$$I = \int \sin x \cos x \, \mathrm{d}x = \sin^2 x - \int \cos x \sin x \, \mathrm{d}x + c$$

$$= \sin^2 x - I + c$$
$$\implies 2I = \sin^2 x + c$$
$$\implies I = \tfrac{1}{2} \sin^2 x + K \qquad (\text{where } K = \tfrac{1}{2}c)$$

(b) $\dfrac{\mathrm{d}}{\mathrm{d}x} (\tfrac{1}{2} \sin^2 x) = \tfrac{1}{2} \times 2 \sin x \cos x = \sin x \cos x$

$$\implies \int \sin x \cos x \, \mathrm{d}x = \tfrac{1}{2} \sin^2 x + c$$

Also, $\sin x \cos x = \tfrac{1}{2} \sin 2x$

Hence, $\displaystyle\int \sin x \cos x \, \mathrm{d}x = \int \tfrac{1}{2} \sin 2x \, \mathrm{d}x = -\tfrac{1}{4} \cos 2x + c$

$$= -\tfrac{1}{4}(1 - 2 \sin^2 x) + c = -\tfrac{1}{4} + \tfrac{1}{2} \sin^2 x + c = \tfrac{1}{2} \sin^2 x + K \qquad (\text{where } K = c - \tfrac{1}{4})$$

5 $\displaystyle\int \ln |x \times 1| \, \mathrm{d}x = \ln x \times x - \int x \times \dfrac{1}{x} \, \mathrm{d}x$

$$= x \ln x - \int 1 \, \mathrm{d}x$$
$$= x \ln x - x + c$$

$$\int_2^3 \ln x \, \mathrm{d}x = \Big[x \ln x - x \Big]_2^3$$

$$\approx 0.910$$

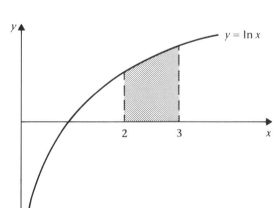

Integrating the circle

1 A circle of radius 1 unit has area π. A quarter of the circle therefore has area $\frac{1}{4}\pi$.

2 (a) $\dfrac{du}{dx} = -2x$ and the integral therefore becomes:

$$\int \sqrt{u} \times -\frac{1}{2x}\, du = -\tfrac{1}{2} \int \frac{\sqrt{u}}{\sqrt{(1-u)}}\, du$$

The integral has not been simplified.

(b) $x = \sin\theta \;\Rightarrow\; \dfrac{dx}{d\theta} = \cos\theta$

$$\int \sqrt{(1-x^2)}\, dx = \int \sqrt{(1-\sin^2\theta)} \times \cos\theta\, d\theta$$

$$= \int \cos^2\theta\, d\theta$$

$$= \tfrac{1}{2}\int (1 + \cos 2\theta)\, d\theta$$

$$= \tfrac{1}{2}(\theta + \tfrac{1}{2}\sin 2\theta) + c$$

$$= \tfrac{1}{2}\theta + \tfrac{1}{2}\sin\theta\cos\theta + c$$

$$= \tfrac{1}{2}\sin^{-1}x + \tfrac{1}{2}x\sqrt{(1-x^2)} + c$$

(c) $\displaystyle\int_0^1 (1-x^2)\, dx = \tfrac{1}{2}\sin^{-1}1 = \tfrac{1}{4}\pi$

$$\int_0^{\frac{1}{2}} \sqrt{(1-x^2)}\, dx = \tfrac{1}{2}\sin^{-1}\tfrac{1}{2} + \tfrac{1}{2}\times\tfrac{1}{2}\sqrt{(1-\tfrac{1}{4})} - \tfrac{1}{2}\sin^{-1}0$$

$$= \tfrac{1}{12}\pi + \tfrac{1}{8}\sqrt{3}$$

3 $\sin 0 = 0$ and $\sin\tfrac{1}{6}\pi = \tfrac{1}{2}$

4 $\displaystyle\int_0^{\frac{1}{6}\pi} \cos^2\theta\, d\theta = \tfrac{1}{2}\int_0^{\frac{1}{6}\pi} (1 + \cos 2\theta)\, d\theta$

$$= \tfrac{1}{2}\left[\theta + \tfrac{1}{2}\sin 2\theta\right]_0^{\frac{1}{6}\pi}$$

$$= \tfrac{1}{12}\pi + \tfrac{1}{4}\sin\tfrac{1}{3}\pi$$

$$= \tfrac{1}{12}\pi + \tfrac{1}{8}\sqrt{3}$$

5 (a) For triangle OAB, $\frac{1}{2} \times$ base $\times$ height $= \frac{1}{2} \times \frac{1}{2} \times \sqrt{\frac{3}{4}} = \frac{1}{8}\sqrt{3}$

$$\text{angle BOC} = \frac{1}{6}\pi$$

and so sector BOC is $\frac{1}{12}$th of the unit circle. Its area is therefore $\frac{1}{12}\pi$.

(b) The shaded area is therefore $\frac{1}{12}\pi + \frac{1}{8}\sqrt{3}$, as established in questions 2(c) and 4.

6 Let $x = 3 \sin \theta \Rightarrow \dfrac{\mathrm{d}x}{\mathrm{d}\theta} = 3 \cos \theta$

$$\int_{1.5}^{3} \sqrt{(9 - x^2)} \,\mathrm{d}x = \int_{\frac{1}{6}\pi}^{\frac{1}{2}\pi} \sqrt{(9 - 9\sin^2 \theta)} \times 3 \cos \theta \,\mathrm{d}\theta$$

$$= 9 \int_{\frac{1}{6}\pi}^{\frac{1}{2}\pi} \cos^2 \theta \,\mathrm{d}\theta$$

$$= \frac{9}{2} \left[\theta + \frac{1}{2}\sin 2\theta \right]_{\frac{1}{6}\pi}^{\frac{1}{2}\pi} = \frac{3}{2}\pi - \frac{9}{8}\sqrt{3}$$

7 $\displaystyle\int \frac{\sec^2 u \,\mathrm{d}u}{1 + \tan^2 u} = \int 1 \,\mathrm{d}u$

$$= u + c = \tan^{-1} x + c$$

8 $\displaystyle\int 1 \,\mathrm{d}u = u + c = \sin^{-1} x + c$

9 $\displaystyle\int -1 \,\mathrm{d}v = -v + C = -\cos^{-1} x + C$

10 (a)

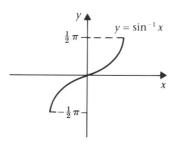

(b)

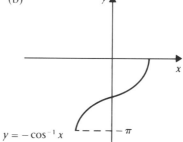

$$\sin^{-1} x = \frac{1}{2}\pi - \cos^{-1} x$$

The answers to questions 8 and 9 are the same if the arbitrary constants are related by $c + \frac{1}{2}\pi = C$.

5 Polynomial approximations

5.1 Taylor's first approximation

> (a) Using radians, obtain values of x and $\sin x$ for small x. For what range of x would you consider $y = x$ to be a reasonable approximation to $y = \sin x$?
>
> (b) Is the approximation '$\sin x \approx x$ for small values of x' valid if x is an angle measured in degrees? Explain your answer.
>
> (c) Find a similar approximation for:
>
>   (i) $\tan x$ (ii) $\cos x$

(a)

x	1	0.5	0.2	0.1	0.01
$\sin x$	0.84	0.479	0.199	0.0998	0.0099998

If you plot the graphs of $y = x$ and $y = \sin x$ on the same axes on a graph plotter, you can see the 'error'.

The percentage error is given by $100\dfrac{x - \sin x}{\sin x}$.

The error function can also be plotted on a graph plotter.

What constitutes a reasonable approximation is open to discussion. The approximation is good for $-0.5 < x < 0.5$ if an error of no more than 5% is considered reasonable.

(b) $y = \sin x$ has gradient function $\dfrac{dy}{dx} = \cos x$ only when measured in radians. Hence $y = x$ is the equation of the tangent at $(0, 0)$ only if x is in radians.

(c) (i) $\tan x \approx x$

    (ii) $\cos x \approx 1$

5.2 The Newton–Raphson method

Show that $f'(a) = \dfrac{f(a)}{a - b}$ and hence that $b = a - \dfrac{f(a)}{f'(a)}$.

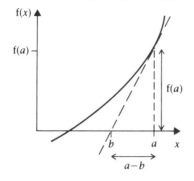

Since $f'(a)$ is the gradient of the graph at $x = a$:

$$\frac{f(a)}{a - b} = f'(a)$$

$$\Rightarrow \quad \frac{f(a)}{f'(a)} = a - b$$

$$\Rightarrow \quad b = a - \frac{f(a)}{f'(a)}$$

5.3 Quadratic approximations

(a) What sort of information is needed to calculate the equation of a quadratic function?

(b) How many different quadratic functions, $p(x) = a + bx + cx^2$, can you find which pass through the point $(0, 10)$ with gradient 4?

(a) You need two pieces of information to define a linear graph. It seems logical to assume that you need three pieces of information to define a quadratic graph, and this is indeed the case.

If, for example, you know that the graph passes through three points, $(-2, 14)$, $(0, 30)$ and $(3, 24)$, and if you let the equation of the graph be $f(x) = a + bx + cx^2$, you can find three simultaneous equations in the three unknowns a, b and c.

If, on the other hand, you know that the graph passes through two specified points and if you also know the gradient of the graph at one of the points, again you have three pieces of information and can therefore deduce the equation of the graph.

These are two ways in which a set of three conditions can define a quadratic function. An alternative set of three conditions is the values of y, $\dfrac{dy}{dx}$ and $\dfrac{d^2y}{dx^2}$ at a single point.

(b) There is an infinite number.

Since $f(0) = 10$, $a + b \times 0 + c \times 0^2 = 10 \Rightarrow a = 10$

$f'(x) = b + 2cx$ and since $f'(0) = 4$, $b + 2c \times 0 = 4 \Rightarrow b = 4$

Thus $f(x) = 10 + 4x + cx^2$ and each value of c gives a different function.

5.4 Maclaurin's series

(a) Compare the function e^x and its derivatives at $x = 0$ with $1 + x + \frac{1}{2}x^2$ and its derivatives at $x = 0$.

(b) Even better approximations can be obtained with cubics. What do you think are the properties of a cubic approximation?

(c) What would be the properties of a fourth degree, a fifth degree and an nth degree approximation?

(a) $f(x) = e^x$, $\quad p(x) = 1 + x + \frac{1}{2}x^2$

$f(0) = 1 = p(0)$

$f'(x) = e^x$, $\quad p'(x) = 1 + x$

$f'(0) = 1 = p'(0)$

$f''(x) = e^x$, $\quad p''(x) = 1$

$f''(0) = 1 = p''(0)$

Thus a quadratic approximation to e^x at $x = 0$ is a quadratic which passes through $(0, 1)$ and has the same gradient and second derivative as e^x.

(b) The cubic approximation will be a function which passes through the point and has the same gradient, the same second derivative and the same third derivative as the function.

(c) Higher order polynomial approximations are possible if the function being approximated can be differentiated repeatedly at a point. You would, for example, have to differentiate a function five times at a point to calculate the fifth degree approximation.

The Newton–Raphson method

1 (a) $f'(x) = 2x - 3\cos x$

(b) $b = a - \dfrac{a^2 - 3\sin a}{2a - 3\cos a}$

If $a = 2$, $b = 2 - \dfrac{2^2 - 3\sin 2}{2 \times 2 - 3\cos 2} = 1.7576$ (Remember to work in radians.)

(c) If $a = 1.7576$, $b = 1.7576 - \dfrac{1.7576^2 - 3\sin 1.7576}{2 \times 1.7576 - 3\cos 1.7576} = 1.7228915$

(d) Now take $a = 1.7228915$ giving $b = 1.7221255$
then $a = 1.7221255$ and $b = 1.7221251$
and finally $a = 1.7221251$ gives $b = 1.7221251$

Thus, two successive values agree to 7 decimal places and you can conclude that the root is 1.722125 (to 6 decimal places).

2

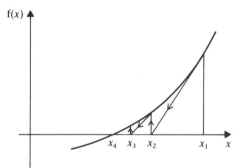

3 (a)

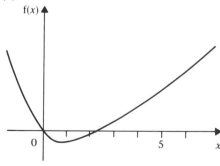

(b) From the graph, the root lies between 2 and 3.

Any value greater than 1 will work, for example, $x_1 = 3$.

(c) $f'(x) = 2x - 6e^{-x}$

$$x_{n+1} = x_n - \frac{x_n^2 - 6 + 6e^{-x_n}}{2x_n - 6e^{-x_n}}$$

(d) $x_1 = 3$, $x_2 = 2.421\,406$, $x_3 = 2.329\,530$, $x_4 = 2.326\,890$, $x_5 = 2.326\,890$
$\Rightarrow x = 2.3269$ to 4 decimal places

4

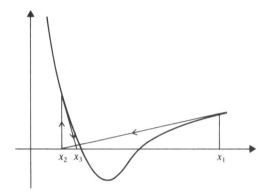

The Newton–Raphson process will not converge to the nearest root.

5E (a) $x = 3.8730$ to 4 decimal places

(b) All values greater than 2.87 will give the root 3.8730.

(c) Any start position between -0.67 and 2.87 will give the root $x = 2$.

(d) If $x_1 = -0.68$ it gives the root 3.87.

If $x_1 = -0.69$ it gives the root -3.87.

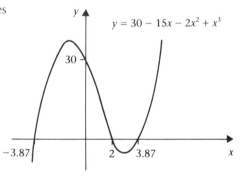

$y = 30 - 15x - 2x^2 + x^3$

You cannot always predict to which root an iteration will converge. If the starting position is reasonably close to the root, you will usually home in on the root very quickly. However, if the iteration takes you near a turning point, then the method becomes very unpredictable. In this case, the method takes you near the turning point at $x = 3$.

(e)

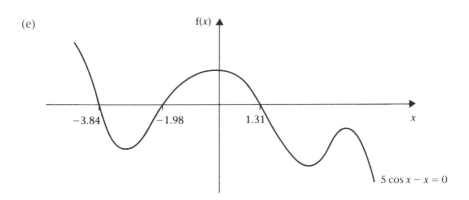

$5 \cos x - x = 0$

From an initial value of -1, the iteration quickly converges to the root -1.977. However, a starting value of -0.5 is near a turning point and the iteration converges to the root -3.837 and not -1.98, the nearest root. Starting values of -7 and -6.5 are some way from any of the roots, as well as being near turning points. In each case, the root which is eventually reached is difficult to predict and depends upon the accuracy of your calculator.

(f)

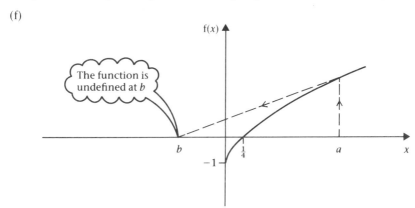

The function is undefined at b

This is an equation which is easily solved by simple algebraic manipulation and you would not normally use the Newton–Raphson method to solve it. It does, however, illustrate how the method can fail to work even if the starting value is not near a turning point. In this case, a starting value must be chosen near the root $\frac{1}{4}$.

6E The graph looks like a standard sine curve, but when you zoom in you see that it has several small turning points very close to each other. To solve this equation you must have a starting point very close to the root you are trying to find.

41

Finding the polynomial

1 $p(0) = 12 \Rightarrow a = 12$
$p'(0) = 11 \Rightarrow b = 11$
$p''(0) = 10 \Rightarrow 2c = 10$
$p^{(3)}(0) = 6 \Rightarrow 6d = 6$

Hence $a = 12, \quad b = 11, \quad c = 5, \quad d = 1$

2 If $p(x) = a + bx + cx^2 + dx^3$

$p(0) = a \quad \Rightarrow a = p(0)$
$p'(0) = b \quad \Rightarrow b = p'(0)$
$p''(0) = 2c \Rightarrow c = p'(0) \div 2$
$p^{(3)}(0) = 6d \Rightarrow d = p^{(3)}(0) \div 6$

Hence $p(x) = p(0) + p'(0)x + p''(0)\dfrac{x^2}{2} + p^{(3)}(0)\dfrac{x^3}{2}$

3 If $p(x)$ is a polynomial of degree four then:

$p(x) = a + bx + cx^2 + dx^3 + ex^4 \Rightarrow$
$\begin{aligned} p'(x) &= b + 2cx + 3dx^2 + 4ex^3 \\ p''(x) &= \qquad\quad 2c + 6dx + 12ex^2 \\ p^{(3)}(x) &= \qquad\qquad\qquad 6d + 24ex \\ p^{(4)}(x) &= \qquad\qquad\qquad\qquad 24e \end{aligned}$

$\Rightarrow \begin{aligned} p(0) &= a \\ p'(0) &= b \\ p''(0) &= 2c \\ p^{(3)}(0) &= 6d \\ p^{(4)}(0) &= 24e \end{aligned}$

But $24 = 4 \times 3 \times 2 \times 1$ is usually written as 4! (called 'factorial four').
So $e = p^{(4)}(0) \div 4!$
In a similar way, $d = p^{(3)}(0) \div 3!$ and $c = p''(0) \div 2!$
Hence $p(x) = p(0) + p'(0)x + p''(0)\dfrac{x^2}{2!} + p^{(3)}(0)\dfrac{x^3}{3!} + p^{(4)}(0)\dfrac{x^4}{4!}$

4 (a) $p(x) = p(0) + p'(0)x + p''(0)\dfrac{x^2}{2!} + p^{(3)}(0)\dfrac{x^3}{3!} + p^{(4)}(0)\dfrac{x^4}{4!} + p^{(5)}(0)\dfrac{x^5}{5!}$

   (b) $p(x) = p(0) + p'(0)x + p''(0)\dfrac{x^2}{2!} + p^{(3)}(0)\dfrac{x^3}{3!} + p^{(4)}(0)\dfrac{x^4}{4!} + \ldots + p^n(0)\dfrac{x^n}{n!}$

5 $f(x) = e^{2x} \Rightarrow f'(x) = 2e^{2x}$
$\qquad\qquad\quad f''(x) = 2^2e^{2x}$
$\qquad\qquad\quad f^{(3)}(x) = 2^3e^{2x}$
$\qquad\qquad\quad f^{(4)}(x) = 2^4e^{2x}$

$\qquad \Rightarrow f(0) = 1$
$\qquad\qquad f'(0) = 2$
$\qquad\qquad f''(0) = 2^2$
$\qquad\qquad f^{(3)}(0) = 2^3$
$\qquad\qquad f^{(4)}(0) = 2^4$

The polynomial:

$$1 + 2x + \frac{2^2x^2}{2!} + \frac{2^3x^3}{3!} + \frac{2^4x^4}{4!}$$

will pass through the same point with the same gradient, and with the same second derivative, third derivative and fourth derivative as the function e^{2x} does when $x = 0$.

Hence it is a good approximation to e^{2x} for values of x near $x = 0$ and this is confirmed by plotting the functions. The approximation gives a percentage error of $\pm 1\%$ for $0.45 < x < 0.64$.

Some proofs

3E

1 (a) ln 0 is undefined.

(b) Since f(0) cannot be found, it is not possible to find a Maclaurin's series. Geometrically, it is not possible to approximate a function at a point that is not defined!

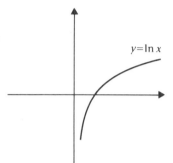

$y = \ln x$

2 (a) $f'(x) = \dfrac{1}{1+x}$

(b) $f''(x) = -1(1+x)^{-2} = -(1+x)^{-2}$

(c) $f^{(3)}(x) = -(-2)(1+x)^{-3} = 2(1+x)^{-3}$
$f^{(4)}(x) = 2 \times -3(1+x)^{-4} = -3!\,(1+x)^{-4}$
$f^{(5)}(x) = 4!\,(1+x)^{-5}$

(d) $f(0) = 0;\quad f'(0) = 1;\quad f''(0) = -1;\quad f^{(3)}(0) = 2;\quad f^{(4)}(0) = -3!;\quad f^{(5)}(0) = 4!$

(e) $\ln(1+x) = 0 + 1x + \dfrac{-1x^2}{2!} + \dfrac{2x^3}{3!} + \dfrac{-3!x^4}{4!} + \dfrac{4!x^5}{5!}$

Note that $\dfrac{2}{3!} = \dfrac{2}{3 \times 2} = \dfrac{1}{3},\ \dfrac{3!}{4!} = \dfrac{3 \times 2 \times 1}{4 \times 3 \times 2 \times 1} = \dfrac{1}{4}$ and $\dfrac{4!}{5!} = \dfrac{1}{5}$

gives $\ln(1+x) = x - \dfrac{x^2}{2} + \dfrac{x^3}{3} - \dfrac{x^4}{4} + \dfrac{x^5}{5} + \ldots$

3 (a) $n(1+x)^{n-1}$

(b) $f''(x) = n(n-1)(1+x)^{n-2}$

$f^{(3)}(x) = n(n-1)(n-2)(1+x)^{n-3}$

(c) $f(0) = 1,\quad f'(0) = n;\quad f''(0) = n(n-1);\quad f^{(3)}(0) = n(n-1)(n-2)$

$(1+x)^n = 1 + nx + \dfrac{n(n-1)}{2!}x^2 + \dfrac{n(n-1)(n-2)}{3!}x^3 + \ldots$

6 First principles

6.1 Zooming in

> P is the point $(3, 3^2)$ and Q has x-coordinate $3 + h$.
>
> (a) What is the y-coordinate of Q?
>
> (b) What is the difference between the y-coordinates of Q and P?
>
> (c) Find the gradient of PQ. (Simplify the expression as far as possible.)
>
> (d) As h becomes smaller and smaller, what happens to the value of the gradient?
>
> (e) What is the advantage of using the letter h rather than a small numerical value?

(a) $(3 + h)^2 = 9 + 6h + h^2$

(b) $6h + h^2$

(c) $\dfrac{6h + h^2}{h} = 6 + h$

(d) The gradient of PQ becomes closer and closer to 6.

(e) The main advantage of using h rather than a particular numerical value is that you have a general answer, $6 + h$, for the gradient PQ, for **any** point Q on the curve. A result like that of part (d) can be seen much more easily from the algebraic expression than it would be from several numerical results. Furthermore, you can see that for **any** small h, the gradient is close to 6. You therefore know that zooming in further (by taking smaller values of h) cannot cause any change in this result: **the graph is locally straight at x = 3 and has gradient 6 at that point.**

Limits

1 (a) -2 (b) 3

2 (a) $\lim\limits_{h\to0} (h + 2) = 2$

(b) $\lim\limits_{h\to0} (5h - 2) = -2$

(c) $\lim\limits_{h\to0} (4h - h^2) = 0$

(d) $\lim\limits_{h\to2} (h + 2) = 4$

(e) $\lim\limits_{h\to-3} \dfrac{2(h - 3)(h + 3)}{h + 3} = \lim\limits_{h\to-3} 2(h - 3)$

$$= -12$$

3 By using smaller and smaller values of h you will probably have convinced yourself of the following results:

(a) $\lim\limits_{h\to0} \dfrac{\sin h}{h} = 1$

(b) $\lim\limits_{h\to0} \dfrac{\cos h - 1}{h} = 0$

(c) $\lim\limits_{h\to0} \dfrac{e^h - 1}{h} = 1$

These results can be demonstrated algebraically, although rigorous proofs are beyond the scope of this unit.